101 ZEN STORIES

by

SENZAKI

CONTENTS

page

1

A CUP OF TEA

Nan-In, a master during the Meiji era, received a university professor who came to inquire about Zen.

Nan-In served tea. He poured his visitor's cup full, and then kept on pouring.

The professor watched the overflow until he no longer could restrain himself. "It is overfull. No more will go in!"

"Like this cup," Nan-In said, "you are full of your own opinions and speculations. How can I show you Zen unless you first empty your cup?"

2

FINDING A DIAMOND ON A MUDDY ROAD

Gu-Do was the Emperor's teacher of his time. Nevertheless he used to travel alone as a wander-

ing mendicant. Once when he was on his way to Edo,
the cultural and political centre of the Shogunate,
he approached a little village named Takenaka. It
was evening and a heavy rain was falling. Gu-Do
was thoroughly wet. His straw sandals were in
pieces. At a farm-house near the village he noticed
four or five pair of sandals in the window and decided
to buy some dry ones.

The woman who offered him the sandals, seeing
how wet he was, invited him to remain for the night
in her home. Gu-Do accepted, thanking her. He
entered and recited a Sutra before the family shrine.
He then was introduced to the woman's mother, and to
her children. Observing that the entire family was
depressed, Gu-Do asked what was wrong.

"My husband is a gambler and a drunkard," the
housewife told him. "When he happens to win he drinks
and becomes abusive. When he losed he borrows money
from others. Sometimes when he becomes thoroughly
drunk, he does not come home at all. What can I do?"

"I will help him," said Gu-Do. "Here is some
money. Get me a gallon of fine wine and something
to eat. Then you may retire. I will meditate before
the shrine."

When the man of the house returned about midnight,
quite drunk, he bellowed, "Hey, wife, I am home. Have
you something for me to eat?"

"I have something for you," said Gu-Do. "I
happened to be caught in the rain and your wife kindly
asked me to remain here for the night. In return, I
have bought some wine and fish so you might as well eat
them."

The man was delighted. He drank the wine at once
and laid himself down on the floor. Gu-Do sat in
meditation beside him.

In the morning when the husband awoke he had
forgotten about the previous night. "Who are you?
Where do you come from?" he asked Gu-Do who still was
meditating.

"I am Gu-Do of Kyoto and I am going on to Edo,"
replied the Zen master.

The man was utterly ashamed. He apologized profusely
to the teacher of his Emperor.

Gu-Do smiled. "Everything in this life is imperma-
nent," he explained. "Life is very brief. If you keep
on gambling and drinking, you will have no time left to
accomplish anything else, and you will cause your family
to suffer too."

The perception of the husband awoke as if from a
dream. "You are right," he declared.

"How can I ever repay you for this wonderful teaching! Let me see you off and carry your things a little way."

"If you wish," assented Gu-Do.

The two started out. After they had gone three miles Gu-Do told him to return. "Just another five miles," he begged Gu-Do. They continued on.

"You may return now," suggested Gu-Do.

"After another ten miles," the man replied.

"Return now," said Gu-Do, when the ten miles had passed.

"Iaam going to follow you all the rest of my life," declared the man.

Modern Zen teachers in Japan all spring from the lineage of a famous master who was the successor of Gu-Do. His name is Mu-Nan, the man who never turned back.

3

IS THAT SO?

The Zen master, Haku-In, was praised by his neighbours as one living a pure life.

A beautiful Japanese girl whose parents owned
a food store lived near him. Suddenly, without a
word, the girl was with child.

This made her parents angry. She would not confess
who the man was, but after much harassment at last
named Haku-In.

In great anger the parents went to the master.
"Is that so?" was all he would say.

After the child was born, it was brought to
Haku-In. By this time he had lost his reputation,
which did not trouble him, but he took very good care
of the child. He obtained milk from his neighbours
and everything that the little one needed.

A year later the girl mother could stand it no
longer. She told her parents the truth that the real
father of the child was a young man who worked in the
fishmarket.

The mother and father of the girl at once went
to Haku-In to ask his forgiveness, to apologize at
length, and to get the child back again.

Haku-In was willing. In yielding, the child all
he said was, "Is that so?"

4

OBEDIENCE

The master Ban-Kei's talks were attended not only
by Zen students but by persons of all ranks and sects.
He never quoted Sutras nor indulged in scholastic
dissertations. Instead his words were spoken directly
from his heart to the hearts of his listeners.

His large audiences angered a priest of the
Nichiren sect because the adherents had left to hear
about Zen. The self-centred Nichiren came to the temple,
determined to debate with Ban-Kei.

"Hey, Zen teacher!" he called out. "Wait a minute.
Whoever respects you will obey what you say, but a man
like myself does not respect you. Can you make me obey
you?"

Come up beside me and I will show you," said Ban-Kei
Proudly the priest pushed his way through the crowd to
the teacher.

Ban-Kei smiled. "Come over to my left side."
The priest obeyed. "No," said Ban-Kei, "we may talk
better if you are on the right side. Step over here."
The priest proudly stepped over to the right.

"You see," observed Ban-Kei, "you are obeying me
and I think you are a very gentle person. Now sit
down and listen."

5

IF YOU LOVE, LOVE OPENLY

Twenty monks and one nun, who was named E-Shun,
were practising meditation with a certain Zen master.

E-Shun was very pretty even though her head was
shaved and here dress plain. Several monks secretly
fell in love with her. One of them wrote her an
endearing letter, insisting upon a private meeting.

E-Shun did not reply. The following day the
master gave a lecture to the group and when it was
over, E-Shun arose. Addressing the one who had
written her, she said, "If you really love me so much,
come and embrace me now."

6

NO LOVINGKINDNESS

There was an old woman in China who had supported
a monk for over twenty years. She had built a little
hut for him and fed him while he was meditating. Finally
she wondered just what progress he had made in all this
time.

To find out, she obtained the help of a girl
rich in desire. "Go and embrace him," she told her,
"and then ask him suddenly, 'What now?'"

The girl called upon the monk and without much
ado caressed him, asking him what he was going to do
about it.

"An old tree grows on a cold rock in winter," replied
the monk somewhat poetically. "Nowhere is there any
warmth."

The girl returned and related what he had said.

"To think I fed that fellow for twenty years!"
exclaimed the old woman in anger. "He showed no con-
sideration for your need, no disposition to explain
your condition. He need not have responded to passion,
but at least he should have evidenced some compassion."

She at once went to the hut of the monk and burned
it down.

7

ANNOUNCEMENT

Tan-Zan wrote sixty postal cards on the last day
of his life, and asked an attendant to mail them. Then
he passed away.

The cards read:

I am departing from this world.

This is my last announcement.

TAN-ZAN.

July 27, 1892.

8

GREAT WAVES

In the early days of the Meiji era there lived a
well-known wrestler called O*Nami, Great Waves.

O-Nami was immensely strong and knew the

art of wrestling. In his private bouts he defeated
even his teacher, but in public he was so bashful that
his own pupils threw him.

O-Nami felt he should go to a Zen master for help.
Haku-Ju, a wandering teacher, was stopping in a little
temple nearby, so O-Nami went to see him and told him
of his trouble.

"Great Waves is your name," the teacher advised,
"so stay in this temple to-night. Imagine that you are
those billows. You are no longer a wrestler who is
afraid. You are those huge waves sweeping everything
before them, swallowing all in their path. Do this and
you will be the greatest wrestler in he land."

The teacher retired. O-Nami sat in meditation try-
ing to imagine himself as waves. He thought of many
different things. Then gradually he turned more and
more to the feeling of the waves. As the night advanced
the waves became larger and larger. They swept away the
flowers in their vases. Even the Buddha in the shrine
was inundated. Before dawn the temple was nothing but
the ebb and flow of an immense sea.

In the morning the teacher found O-Nami meditating,
a faint smile on his face. He patted the wrestler's
shoulder. "Now nothing can disturb you," he said. "You

are these waves. You will sweep everything before you."

The same day O-Nami entered contests and won.
After that, no one in Japan was able to defeat him.

9

THE MOON CANNOT BE STOLEN

Ryo-Kwan, a Zen master, lived the simplest kind
of life in a little hut at the foot of a mountain.
One evening a theif visited the hut only to discover
there was nothing in it to steal.

Ryo-Kwan returned and caught him. "You may have
come a long way to visit me," he told the prowler,
"and you should not return empty-handed. Please take
my clothes as a gift."

The theif was bewildered. He took the clothes
and slunk away.

Ryo-Kwan sat naked watching the moon.

"Poor fellow," he mused, "I wish I could give him
this beautiful moon."

10

THE LAST POEM OF HO-SHIN

The Zen master, Ho-Shin, lived in China many
years. Then he returned to the north-eastern part
of Japan where he taught his disciples. When he
was very old, said to his disciples, "I am not going
to be alive next year so you fellows should treat me
well this year."

The pupils thought he was joking, but since
he was a great-hearted teacher, each in turn treated
him to a feast on succeeding days of the departing
year.

On the eve of the new year, Toku-Fu concluded,
"You have been good to me. I shall leave you to-morrow
afternoon when the snow has stopped."

The disciples laughed, thinking he was aging and
talking nonsense since the night was clear and without
snow. But at midnight snow began to fall, and the
next day they did not find their teacher about.

They went to the meditation hall. There he had passed on.

Ho-Shin, who related this story, told his disciples, "it is not necessary for a Zen master to predict his passing, but if he really wishes to do so, he can."

"Can you?" someone asked.

"Yes," answered Ho-Shin. "I will show you what I can do sevendays from now."

None of the disciples believed him, and most of them had even forgotten the conversation when Ho-Shin called them together.

"Seven days ago," he remarked, "I said I was going to leave you. It is customary to write a farewell poem, but I am neither poet nor calligrapher. Let one of you inscribe my last words."

His followers thought he was joking, but one of them started to write.

"Are you ready?" Ho-Shin asked.

"Yes, sir," replied the writer.

Then Ho-Shin dictated,

> I came from brilliancy
>
> And return to brilliancy.
>
> What is this?

The poem was one line short of the customary four,

so the disciple said, "Master, we are one line short."

Ho-Shin, with the roar of a conquering lion,
shouted, "Kaa!" and was gone.

11

THE STORY OF SHUN-KAI

The exquisite Shun-Kai whose other name was Suzu
was compelled to marry against her wishes when she was
quite young. Later, after this marriage had ended,
she attended the university where she studied
philosophy.

To see Shun-Kai was to fall in love with her.
Moreover, wherever she herself went, she fell in
love with others. Love was with her at the university
and afterwards, when philosophy did not satisfy her
and she visited a temple to learn about Zen, the Zen
sutdents fell in love with her. Shun-Kai's whole
life was saturated with love.

At last in Kyoto she became a real student of
Zen. Her brothers in the sub-temple of Ken-Nin
praised her sincerity. One of them proved to be a
congenial spirit and assisted her in the mastery of Zen.

The abbot of Ken-Nin, Moku-Rai, Silent Thunder,
was severe. He kept the precepts himself and ex-
pected his priests to do so. In modern Japan
whatever zeal these priests have lost for Buddhism
they seem to have gained for having wives. Moku-
Rai used to take a broom and chase the women away
when he found them in any of his temples, but the
more wives he swept out, the more seemed to come
back.

In this particular temple, the wife of the
head priest became jealous of Shun-Kai's earnest-
ness and beauty. Hearing the students praise her
serious Zen made this wife squirm and itch.
Finally she spread a rumour about Shun-Kai and
the young man who was her friend. As a conse-
quence, he was expelled, and Shun-Kai was removed
from the temple.

"I may have made the mistake of love,"
thought Shun-Kai, "but the priest's wife shall not
remain in the temple either if my friend is to be
treated so unjustly."

Shun-Kai the same night with a can of kerosene
set fire to the five-hundred year-old temple and

burned it to the ground. In the morning, she
found herself in the hands of the police.

A young lawyer became interested in her, and
endeavoured to make her sentence lighter. "Do not
help me," she told him, "I might decide to do
something else which would only imprison me again."

At last a sentence of seven years was completed,
and Shun-Kai was released from the prison where the
sixty-year-old warden also had become enamoured to
her.

But now everyone looked upon her as a 'jail-
bird.' No one would associate with her. Even the
Zen people who are supposed to believe in enlightenment in this life and with this body, shunned her.
Zen, Shun-Kai found, was one thing, and the followers of Zen, quite another. Her relatives would
have nothing to do with her. She grew sick, poor,
and weak.

She met a Shin-Shu priest who taught her the
name of the Buddha of Love, and in this Shun-Kai
found some solace and peace of mind. She passed
away when she was still exquisitely beautiful and
hardly thirty years old.

She wrote her own story in a futile endeavor
to support herself and some of it she told to a
woman writer. So it reached the Japanese people.

Those who rejected Shun-Kai, those who scandalized
and hated her, now read of her life with tears of
remorse.

12

HAPPY CHINAMAN

Anyone walking about Chinatown in America
will observe statues of a stout fellow carrying
a linenssack. Chinese merchants call him Happy
Chinaman, or Laughing Buddha.

This Ho-Tei lived in the Tang Dynasty. He
had no desire to call himself a Zen master or to
gather many disciples about him. Instead he
walked the streets with a big sack into which he
would put gifts of candy, fruit, or doughnuts.
These he would give to children who gathered
around him in play. He established a kindergarten
of the streets.

Whenever he met a Zen devotee he would extend
his hand and say, "Give me one cent." If anyone
asked him to return to a temple to teach others
he would reply, "Give me one cent."

Once as he was bout his play-work, another
Zen master happened along and inquired, "What
is the significance of Zen?"

Ho-Tei immediately plopped his sack down on
the ground in silent answer.

"Then," asked the other, "what is the ac-
tualization of Zen?"

At once the happy Chinaman swung the sack
over his shoulder and continued on his way.

13

A BUDDHA

In Tokyo in the Meiji era there lived two
prominent teachers of opposite characteristics.
One, Un-Sho, an instructor in Shingon, kept
Buddha's precepts scrupulously. He never drank
intoxicants, nor did he eat after eleven o'clock
in the morning. The other teacher, Tan-Zan, a
professor of philosophy at the Imperial University,
never observed the precepts. When he felt like
eating he ate, and when he felt like sleeping in
the daytime he slept.

One day Un-Sho visited Tan-Zan who was drinking

wine at the time, not even a drop of which is supposed to touch the tongue of a Buddhist.

"Hello, brother," Tan-Zan greeted him. "Won't you have a drink?"

"I never drink!" exclaimed Un-Sho solemnly.

"One who does not drink is not even human," said Tan-Zan.

"Do you mean to call me inhuman just because I do not indulge in intoxicating liquids!" exclaimed Un-Sho in anger. "Then if I am not human, what am I?"

"A Buddha," answered Tan-Zan.

14

MUDDY ROAD

Tan-Zan and Eki-Do were travelling together down a muddy road. A heavy rain was still falling.

Coming around a bend they met a lovely girl in a silk kimono and sash, unable to cross the intersection.

"Come on, girl," said Tan-Zan at once.

Lifting her in his arms, he carried her over the
mud.

Eki-Do did not speak again until that night
when they reached a lodging temple. Then he no
longer could restrain himself. "We monks don't
go near females," he told Tan-Zan, "and especially
young and lovely ones. It is dangerous. Why did
you do that?"

"I left the girl there," said Tan-Zan. "Are
you still carrying her?"

15

SHO-UN AND HIS MOTHER

Sho-Un became a teacher of Soto Zen. When
he was still a student his father passed away,
leaving him to care for his old mother.

When Sho-Un would go to a meditation hall,
he took his mother with him. Since she accompanied
him, when he visited monasteries, he could not live
with the monks. So he would build a little house
and care for her there. He would copy Sutras,
Buddhist verses, and in this manner receive a few
coins for food.

St. Matthew: "And why take ye thought for rainment?
Consider the lilies of the field, how they grow.
They toil not, neither do they spin, and yet I say
unto you that even Solomon in all his glory was not
arrayed like one of these. . . . Take therefore no
thought for the morrow, for the morrow shall take
thought for the tings of itself."

Ga-San said, "Whoever uttered those words,
I consider an enlightened man."

The student continued reading. "Ask and it
shall be given you, seek and ye shall find,
knock and it shall be opened unto you. For everyone that asketh receiveth, and he that seeketh
findeth, and to him that knocketh, it shall be
opened."

Ga-San remarked, "That is excellent. Whoever
said that is not far from Buddhahood."

17

STINGY IN TEACHING

A young physician in Tokyo named Kusuda
met a college friend who had been studying Zen.
The young doctor asked him what Zen was.

"I cannot tell you what it is," the friend replied,
"But one thing is certain. If you understand Zen
you will not be afraid to die."

"That's fine," said Kusuda. "I will try it.
Where can I find a teacher?"

"Go to the master, Nan-In," the friend told him.

So Kusuda went to call on Nan-In. He carried
a dagger nine and a half inches long to determine
whether or not the teacher himself was afraid to die.

When Nan-In saw Kusuda he exclaimed, "Hello,
friend. How are you? We haven't seen each other
for a long time!"

This perplexed Kusuda who replied, "We have
never met before."

"That's right," answered Nan-In. "I mistook
you for another physician who is receiving instruction
here."

With such a beginning, Kusuda lost his chance
to test the master, so reluctantly he asked if he
might receive Zen instruction.

Nan-In said, "Zen is not a difficult task. If
you are a physician, treat your patients with
kindness. That is Zen."

Kusuda visited Nan-In three times. Each
time Nan-In told him the same thing. "A physician

should not waste time around here. Go home and
take care of your patients."

It was not yet clear to Kusuda how such
teaching could remove the fear of death. So on
his fourth visit he complained, "My friend told me
that when one learns Zen one loses his fear of
death. Each time I come here all you tell me is
to take care of my patients. I know that much.
If that is your so-called Zen, I am not going to
visit you any more."

Nan-In smiled and patted the doctor. "I
have been too strict with you. Let me give you
a Ko-An." He presented Kusuda Jo-Shu's Mu to
work over, which is the first mind-enlightening
problem in a book called 'The Gateless Gate'.

Kusuda pondered this problem of Mu (No-
Thing) for two years. At length he thought he
had reached certainty of mind. But his teacher
commented, "You are not in yet."

Kusuda continued in concentration for another
year and a half. His mind became placid. Problems
dissolved. No-Thing became the truth. He served
his patients well and without even knowing it, he
was free from concern over life and death.

Then when he visited Nan-In, his old teacher
just smiled.

18

A PARABLE

Buddha told a parable in a Sutra:

A man travellingacross a field encountered a
tiger. He fled, the tiger after him. Coming to
a precipice, he caught hold of the root of a wild
vine and swung himself down over the edge. The
tiger sniffed at him from above. Trembling, the
man looked down to where, far below, another
tiger was waiting to eat him. Only the vine
sustained him.

Two mince, one white and one black, little by
little, started to gnaw away the vine. The man
saw a luscious strawberry near him. Grasping the
vine with one hand, he plucked the strawberry
with the other. How sweet it tasted!

19

THE FIRST PRINCIPLE

When one goes to O-Baku temple in Kyoto he
sees carved over the gate the words, The First

Principle. The letters are unusually large, and
those who appreciate calligraphy always admire
them as being a masterpiece. They were drawn by
Ko-Sen two hundred years ago.

When the master drew them he did so on paper
from which workmen made the larger carving in
wood. As Ko-Sen sketched the letters, a bold pupil
was with him who had made several gallons of ink
for calligraphy, and who never failed to criticize
his master's work.

"That is not good," he told Ko-Sen after the
first effort.

"How is that one?"

"Poor. Worse than before," pronounced the
pupil.

Ko-Sen patiently wrote one sheet after another
until eighty-four First Principles had accumulated,
still without the approval of the pupil.

Then, when the young man stepped outside for
a few moments, Ko-sen thought, "Now is my chance
to escape his keen eye," and he wrote hurriedly,
with a mind free from distraction, 'The First
Principle.'

"A masterpiece," announced the pupil.

20

A MOTHER'S ADVICE

Ji-Un, a Shingon master, was a well-known
Sanscrit scholar of the Tokugawa era. When he
was young, he used to deliver lectures to his
brother students.

His mother heard about this, and wrote him
a letter:

"Son, I do not think you became a devotee
of the Buddha because you desired to turn into
a walking dictionary for others. There is no end
to information and commentation, glory and honor.
I wish you would stip this lecture business.
Shut yourself up in a little temple in a remote
part of the mountain. Devote your time to
meditation and in this way attain true realization."

21

THE SOUND OF ONE HAND

The master of Ken-Nin temple was Moku-Rai
Silent Thunder. He had a little protege named

Toyo who was only twelve years old. Toyo saw
the older disciples visit the master's room
each morning and evening to receive instruction
in San-Zen or personal guidance in which they
were given Ko-Ans to stop mind-wandering.

Toyo wished to do San-Zen also. "Wait a
while," said Moku-Rai. "You are too young."

But the child insisted, so the teacher finally
consented.

In the evening little Toyo went at the proper
time to the threshold of Moku-Rai's San-Zen room.
He struck the gong to announce his presence, bowed
respectfully three times outside the door, and went
to sit before the master in respectful silence.

"You can hear the sound of two hands when
they clap together," said Moku-Rai. "Now show me
the sound of one hand."

Toyo bowed and went to his room to consider
this problem. From his window he could hear the
music of the Geisha girls. "Ah, I have it!" he
proclaimed.

The next evening when his teacher asked him
to illustrate the sound of one hand, Toyo began to
play the music of the Geishas.

"No, no," siad Moku-Rai. "That will never
do. That is not the sound of one hand."

Thinking that such music might interrupt, Toyo moved his abode to a quiet place. He meditated again. "What can the sound of one hand be?" He happened to hear some water dripping. "I have it," imagined Toyo.

When he appeared before his teacher, Toyo imitated dripping water.

"What is that?" asked Moku-Rai. "That is the sound of dripping water, but not the sound of one hand. Try again."

In vain Toyo meditated to hear the sound of one hand. He heard the sighing of the wind. But the sound was rejected.

He heard the cry of an owl. This also was refused.

The sound of one hand was not the locusts.

For more than ten times Toyo visited Moku-Rai with different sounds. All were wrong. For almost a year he pondered what the sound of one hand might be.

At last little Toyo entered true meditation and transcended all sounds. "I could collect no more," he explained later, "so I reached the soundless sound."

Toyo had realized the sound of one hand.

22

MY HEART BURNS LIKE FIRE

Soyen Shaku, the first Zen teacher to come to
America, said, "My heart burns like fire but my
eyes are as cold as dead ashes." He made the
following rules which he practised every day of
his life:

In the morning before dressing, light incense
and meditate.

Retire at a regular hour. Partake of food at
regular intervals. Eat with moderation and never
to the point of satisfaction.

Receive a guest with the same attitude you
have when alone. When alone, maintain the same
attitude you have in receiving guests.

Watch what you say, and whatever you say,
practise it.

When an opportunity comes, do not let it
pass by, yet always think twice before acting.

Do not regret the past. Look to the future.

Have the fearless attitude of a hero and the
loving heart of a child.

Upon retiring, sleep as if you had entered your

last sleep. Upon awakening, leave your bed
behind you instantly as if you had cast away a
pair of old shoes.

23

E-SHUN'S DEPARTURE

When E-Shun, the Zen nun, was past sixty
and about to leave this world, she asked some
monks to pile up wood in the yard.

Seating herself firmly in the centre of the
funeral pyre, she had it set fire around the edges.

"O, nun!" shouted one monk, "is it hot in
there?"

Such a matter would conern only a stupid
person like yourself," answered E-Shun. The
flames arose, and she passed away.

24

RECITING SUTRAS

A farmer requested a Tendai priest to recite
Sutras for his wife who had died. After the

recitation was over the farmer asked, "Do you
~~think~~ my wife will gain merit from this?"

"Not only your wife, but all sentient beings
will benefit from the recitation of Sutras,"
answered the priest.

"If you say all sentient beings will benefit,"
said the farmer, "my wife may be very weak and
others will take advantage of her, getting the
benefit she should have. So please recite Sutras
just for her."

The priest explained that it was the desire
fo a Buddhist to offer blessings and wish merit for
every living being.

"That is a fine teaching," concluded the farmer,
"but please make one exception. I have a neighbour
who is rough and mean to me. Just exclude him from
all those sentient beings."

25

THREE DAYS MORE

Sui-Wo, the disciple of Haku-In, was a good
teacher. During one summer seclusion period, a
pupil came to him from a southern island of Japan.

Sui-Wo gave him the problem, "Hear the sound of one hand."

The pupil remained three years but could not pass this test. One night he came in tears to Sui-Wo. "I must return south in shame and embarrassment," he said, "for I cannot solve my problem."

"Wait one week more and meditate constantly," advised Sui-Wo. Still no enlightenment came to the pupil. "Try for another week," said Sui-Wo. The pupil obeyed, but in vain.

"Still another week" Yet this was of no avail. In despair the student begged to be released, but Sui-Wo requested another meditation of five days. They were without result. Then he said, "Meditate for three days longer, then if you fail to attain enlightenment, you had better kill yourself."

On the second day the pupil was enlightened.

26

TRADING DIALOGUE FOR LODGING

Provided he makes and wins an argument about Buddhism with those who live there, any wandering

wandering monk can remain in a Zen temple. If
he is defeated, he has to move on.

In a temple in the northern part of Japan, two
brother monks were dwelling together. The elder
one was learned, but the younger one was stupid and
had but one eye.

A wandering monk came and asked for lodging,
properly challenging to debate about the sublime
teaching. The elder brother, tired that day from
much studying, told the younger one to take his
place. "Go and request the dialogue in silence,"
he cautioned.

So the young monk and the stranger went to
the shrine and sat down.

Shortly afterwards the traveller rose and went
in to the elder brother and said, "Your young
brother is a wonderful fellow. He defeated me."

"Relate to me the dialogue," said the elder
one.

"Well," explained the traveller, "first I held
up one finger, representing Buddha, the enlightened
one. So he held up two fingers, signifying Buddha
and his teaching. I held up three fingers, representing Buddha, his teaching, and his followers,
living the harmonious life. Then he shook his clenched
fist in my face, indicating that all three come from
one realization. Thus, he won and so I have no right

to remain here." With this the traveller left.

"Where is that fellow?" asked the younger
one, running in to his elder brother.

"I understand you won the debate."

"Won nothing. I'm going to beat him up."

"Tell me the subject of the debate," asked
the elder one.

"Why, the minute he saw me he held up one
finger, insulting me by insinuating that I have
only one eye. Since he was a stranger, I thought
I would be polite to him and hold up two fingers
congratulating him that he has two eyes. Then
the impolite wretch held up three fingers, suggest-
ing that between us we only have three eyes. So,
I got mad and started to punch him, but he ran out
and that ended it!"

27

THE VOICE OF HAPPINESS

After Ban-Kei had passed away, a blind man
who lived near the master's temple told a friend:
"Since I am blind, I cannot watch a person's

face, so I must judge his character by the sound
of his voice. Ordinarily when I hear someone
congratulate another upon his happiness or success,
I hear a secret tone of envy. When condolence is
expressed for the misfortune of another, I hear
pleasure and satisfaction, as if the one condoling
was really glad there was something left to gain
in his own world.

"In all my experience, however, Ban-Kei's
voice was always sincere. Whenever he expressed
happiness, I heard nothing but happiness, and
whenever he expressed sorrow, sorrow was all I
heard."

28

OPEN YOUR OWN TREASURE HOUSE

Dai-Ju visited the master, Ba-So, in China.
Ba-So asked, "What do you seek?"

"Enlightenment," replied Dai-Ju.

"You have your own treasure house. Why do
you search outside?" Ba-So asked.

Dai-Ju inquired, "Where is my treasure
house?"

Ba-So answered, "What you are asking is your treasure house."

Dai-Ju was enlightened! Ever after he urged his friends, "Open your own treasure house and use those treasures."

29

NO WATER, NO MOON

When the nun, Chiyono, studied Zen under Bukko of Engaku, she was unable to attain the fruits of meditation for a long time.

At last one moonlit night she was carrying water in an old pail bound with bamboo. The bamboo broke and the bottom fell out of the pail, and at that moment, Chiyono was set free!

In commemoration, she wrote a poem:

In this way and that I tried to save the old pa
Since the bamboo strip was weakening and about
      to break
Until at last the bottom fell out.
No more water in the pail!
No more moon in the water!

30

CALLING CARD

Kei-Chu, the great Zen teacher of the Meiji era, was the head of Tofuki, a cathedral in Kyoto. Oneday the governor of Kyoto called upon him for the first time.

His attendant presented the card of the governor, which read: Kitagaki, Governor of Kyoto.

"I have no business with such a fellow," said Kei-Chu to his attendant. "Tell him to get out of here."

The attendant carried the card back with apologies. "That was my erroe," said the governor as with a pencil he scratched the words, Governor of Kyoto. "Ask your teacher again."

"Oh, is that Kitagaki?" exclaimed the teacher when he saw the card. "I want to see that fellow."

31

EVERYTHING IS BEST

When Ban-Zan was walking through a market,
he overheard a conversation between a butcher and
his customer.

"Give me the best piece of meat you have,"
said the customer.

"Everything in my shop is the best," replied
the butcher. "You cannot find here any piece of
meat that is not the best."

Ban-Zan at these words became enlightened.

32

INCH TIME FOOT GEM

A lord asked Taku-An, a Zen teacher, to
suggest how he might pass the time. He felt
his days very long attending his office and
sitting stiffly to receive the homage of others.

Taku-An wrote eight Chinese letters and gave
them to theman.

     Not twice this day

     Inoh time foot gem.

     This day will not come again.

     Each minute is worth a priceless gem.

33

MOKU-SEN'S HAND

Moku-Sen Hiki was living in a temple in the
state ofTanba. One of his adherents complained
of the stinginess of his wife.

Moku-Sen visited the adherent's wife and
showed her his clenched fist before her face.

"What do you mean by that?" asked the
surprised woman.

"Suppose my fist were always like that. What
would you call it?" he asked.

"Deformed," replied the woman.

Then he opened his hand flat in her face and
asked, "Suppose it were always like that. What then?"

"Another kind of deformity," siad the wife.

"If you understand that much," finished
Moku-Sen, "you are a good wife." Then he left.

After his visit, this wife helped her husband
to distribute as well as to save.

34

A SMILE IN HIS LIFETIME

Moku-Gen was never known to smile until his
last day on earth. When his time came to pass
away he said to his faithful ones, "You have studied
under me for more than ten years. Show me your
real interpretation of Zen. Whoever expresses
this most clearly shall be my successor, and
receive my robe and bowl."

Everyone watched Moku-Gen's severe face,
but no one answered.

En-Cho, a disciple who had been with his
teacher for a long time, moved near the bedside.
He pushed forwardthe medicine cup a few inches.
This was his answer to the command.

The teacher's face became even more severe.
"Is that all you understand?" he asked.

En-Cho reached out and moved the cup back
again.

A beautiful smile broke over the features of
Moku-Gen. "You rascal," he told En-Cho. "You
worked with me ten years and have not yet seen my
whole body. Take the robe and bowl. They belong
to you."

35

EVERY MINUTE ZEN

Zen students are with their masters at least
ten years before they presume to teach others.
Nan-In was visited by Ten-No who, having passed
his apprenticeship, had become a teacher. The
day happened to be rainy, so Ten- No wore wooden
shoes and carried an umbrella. After greeting
him, Nan-In remarked, "I suppose you left your
wooden shoes in the vestibule. I want to know
if your umbrella is on the right or left side of
the shoes."

Ten-No, confused, had no instant answer.

He realized that he was unable to carry his Zen
every minute. He became Nan-In's pupil, and
studied six more years to accomplish his every-
minute Zen.

36

FLOWE SHOWER

Subhuti was Buddha's disciple. He was able
to understand the potency of emptiness, the viewpoint that nothing exists except in its relation-
ship of subjectivity and objectivity.

One day Subhuti in a mood of sublime emptiness, was sitting under a tree. Flowers began to
fall about him.

"We are praising you for your discourse on
emptiness," the gods whispered to him.

"But I have not spoken of emptiness, we have
not heard emptiness," responded the gods. "This
is the true emptiness." And blossoms showered
upon Subhuti as rain.

37

PUBLISHING THE SUTRAS

Tetsu-Gen, a devotee of Zen in Japan, decided
publish the Sutras which at that time were available
only in Chinese. The books were to be printed with
wood blocks in an edition of seven thousand copies
a tremendous undertaking.

Tetsu-Gen began by travelling and collecting
donations for this purpose. A few sympathizers
would give him a hundred ryo, but most of the time
he received only small coins. He thanked each
donor with equal gratitude. After ten years
Tetsu-Gen had enough money to begin his task.

It happened that at that time the Uji river
overflowed. Famine followed. Tetsu-Gen took
the funds he had collected for the books and spent
them to save others from starvation. Then he again
began his work of collecting.

Several years afterwards an epidemic spread
over the country. Tetsu-Gen again gave away what
he had collected, to help his people.

For a third time he started his work, and after
twenty years his wish was fulfilled. The printing
blocks which produced the first edition of Sutras

can be seen to-day in the Obaku monastery in
Kyoto.

The Japanese tell their children that Tetsu-Gen
made three sets of Sutras, and that the first two
invisible sets surpass even the last.

38
GI-SHO'S WORK

Gi-Sho was ordained as a nun when she was
ten yearsold. She received training just as the
little boys did. When she reached the age of
sixteen, she travelled from one Zen master to
another, studying with them all.

She remained three years with Un-Zan, six
years with Gu-Kei, but was unable to obtain a
clear vision. At last she went to the master
In-Zan.

In-Zan showed her no distinction at all on
account of her sex. He scolded her like a thunder-
storm. He cuffed her to awaken her inner nature.
Gi-Sho remained with In-Zan thirteen years, and then
she found that which she was seeking!

In her honour, In-Zan wrote a poem:

> This nun studied thirteen years under my guidance.
> In the evening she considered the deepest Ko-Ans,
> In the morning she was wrapped in other Ko-Ans.
> The Chinese nun, Tetsu-Ma, surpassed all before her,
> And since Mu-Jaku, none has been so genuine as
>   this Gi-Sho!
>   Yet there are many more gates for her to
>   pass through.
>   She should receive still more blows from my
>   iron fist.

After Gi-Sho was enlightened, she went to the
province of Banshu, started her own Zen temple, and
taught two hundred other nuns until she passed
away in the month of August.

39

SLEEPING IN THE DAYTIME

The master, Soyen Shaku, passed from this
world when he was sixty-one years of age. Ful-
filling his life's work, he left a great teaching,
far richer than that of most Zen masters. His
used to sleep in the daytime during mid-
while he overlooked this, he himself

When he was but twelve years old he was already
studying Tendai, philosophical speculation. One
summer day the air had been so sultry that little
Soyen stretched his legs and want to sleep while
his teacher was away.

Three hours passed when suddenly he, waking,
heard his master enter, but it was too late. There
he lay, sprawled across the doorway.

"I beg your pardon, I beg your pardon," his
teacher whispered, stepping carefully over Soyen's
body as if it were that of some distinguished guest.
After this, Soyen never slept again in the afternoon.

40

IN DREAMLAND

"Our schoolmaster used to take a nap every
afternoon," related a disciple of Soyen Shaku.
"We children asked him why he did it and he
told us, 'I go to dreamland to meet the old
sages just as Confucius did.' When Confucius slept,
he would dream of ancient sages and later tell
his followers about them.

"It was extremely hot one day, so some of us
took a nap. Our schoolmaster scolded us. 'We went
dreamland to meet the ancient sages the same as
Confucius did,' we explained. 'What was the
message from those sages?' our schoolmaster demanded
One of us replied, 'We went to dreamland and met the
sages and asked them if our schoolmaster came there
every afternoon, but they said they had never seen
any such fellow.' "

41

JO-SHU'S ZEN

Jo-Shu began the study of Zen when he was
sixty years old and continued until he was eighty,
when he realized Zen.

He taught from the age of eighty until he
was one hundred and twenty.

A student once asked him, "If I haven't
anyting in my mind, what shall I do?"

Jo-Shu replied, "Throw it out."

"But if I haven't anything, how can I throw
it out?" continued the questioner.

"Well," said Jo-Shu, "then carry it out."

42

THE DEAD MAN'S ANSWER

When Maniya, who later became a well-known
preacher, went to a teacher for personal guidance,
he asked to explain the sound of one hand.

Mamiya concentrated upon what the sound of
one hand might be. "You are not working hard
enough," his teacher told him. "You are too attached
to food, wealth, things, and that sound. It would
be better if you died. That would solve the
problem."

The next time Mamiya appeared before his
teacher he was again asked what he had to show
regarding the sound of one hand. Mamiya at
once fell over as if he were dead.

"You are dead all right," observed the
teacher. "But how about that sound?"

"I haven't solved that yet," replied
Mamiya, looking up.

"Dead men do not speak," said the teacher.
"Get out!"

43

ZEN IN A BEGGAR'S LIFE

To-Sui was a well-known Zen teacher of his
time. He had lived in several temples and taught
in various provinces.

The last temple he visited accumulated so
many adherents that To-Sui told them he was
going to quit the lecture business entirely. He
advised them to disperse and to go wherever they
desired. After that, no one could find any trace
of him.

Three years later one of his disciples discovered
him living with some beggars under a bridge in
Kyoto. He at once implored To-Sui to teach him.

"If you can do as I do for even a couple of
days, I might," To-Sui replied.

So the former disciple dressed as a beggar and
spent a day with To-Sui. The following day one of
the beggars died. To-Sui and his pupil carried the
body off at midnight and buried it on a mountain-
side. After that they returned to their shelter
under the bridge.

To-Sui slept soundly the remainder of the
night, but the disciple could not sleep. When

morning came To-Sui said, "We do not have to beg
food to-day. Our dead friend has left some over
there." But the disciple was unable to eat a
single bite of it.

"I have said you could not do as I, "
concluded To-Sui. "Get out of here and do not
bother me again."

44

THE THIEF WHO BECAME A DISCIPLE

One evening as Shichiri Ko-Jun was reciting
Sutras, a thief with a sharp sword entered,
demanding either his money or his life.

Shichiri told him, "Do not disturb me. You
can find the money in that drawer." Then he
resumed his recitation.

A little while afterward he stopped and called,
"Don't take it all. I need some to pay taxes with
to-morrow."

The intruder gathered up most of the money
and started to leave. "Thank a person when you
receive a gift," Shichiri added. The man thanked
him and made off.

A few days afterwards the fellow was caught
and confessed, among others, the offence against
Shichiri. When Shichiri was called as a witness,
he said, "This man is no thief, at least as far as
I am concerned. I gave him the money and he thanked
me for it."

After he had finished his prison term, the man
went to Shichiri and became his disciple.

45

RIGHT AND WRONG

When Ban-Kei held his seclusion -weeks of
meditation, pupils from many parts of Japan came
to attent. During one of these gatherings a
pupil was caught stealing. The matter was
reported to Ban-Kei, with the request that the
culprit be expelled. Ban-Kei ignored the case.

Later the pupil was caught in a similar act,
and again Ban-Kei disregarded the matter. This
angered the other pupils who drew up a petition
asking for the dismissal of the thief, stating that
otherwise they would leave in a body.

When Ban-Kei had read the petition, he called

everyone before him. "You are wise brothers,"
he told them. "You know what is right and what
is not right. You may go somewhere else to study
if you wish, but this poor brother does not even
know right from wrong. Who will teach him if I
do not? I am going to keep him here even if all
the rest of you leave."

A torrent of tears cleansed the face of the
brother who had stolen. All desire to thieve had
vanished.

46

HOW GRASS AND TREES BECOME ENLIGHTENED

During the Kamakura period, Shin-Kwan studied
Tendai six years, then studied Zen seven years,
then he went to China, and contemplated Zen for
thirteen years more.

When he returned to Japan, many desired to
interview him, and asked obscure questions.
But when Shin-Kwan received visitors, which was
infrequently, he seldom answered their questions.

One day a fifty-year-old student of Enlightenment said to Shin-Kwan, "I have studied the Tendai
school of thought since I was a little boy, but
one thing in it I cannot understand. Tendai
claims that even the grass and trees will become
enlightened. To me this seems very strange."

"Of what use is it ot discuss how grass and
trees become enlightened?" asked Shin-Kwan.

"The question is how you yourself can become
so. Did you ever consider that?"

"I never thought of it in that way," marvelled
the old man.

"Then go home and think it over," finished
Shin-Kwen.

47

THE STINGY ARTIST

Gessen was an artist monk. Before he would
start a drawing or painting, he always insisted
upon being paid in advance, and his fees were high
He was known as the 'stingy artist'.

A geisha girl once gave him a commission
for a painting. "How much can you pay?" inquired
Gessen.

"Whateve you charge," replied the girl,
but I want you to do the work in front of me."

So on a certain day Gessen was called by the
Geisha. She was holding a feast for her patron.

Gessen with fine brush work did the painting.
When it was completed he asked the highest sum of
his time.

He received his pay. Then the Geisha turned
to her patron, saying, "All this artist wants is
money. His paintings are fine but his mind is
dirty, money has caused it to become muddy. Drawn
by such a filthy mind, his work is not fit to
exhibit. It is just about good enough for one of
my petticoats.

Removing her skirt, she then asked Gessen to
do another picture on the back of her petticoat.

"How much will you pay?" asked Gessen.

"Oh, any amount," answered the girl.

Gessen named a fancy price, painted the picture
in the manner requested and went away.

It was learned later that Gessen had these
reasons for desiring money. A ravaging famine
often visited his province. The rich would not
help the poor, a Gessen had a secret warehouse
unknown to anyone, which he kept filled with grain,
prepared for these emergencies.

From his village to the National Shrine, the
road was in very poor condition and many travellers
suffered while traversing it. He desired to build
a better road.

His teacher had passed away without realizing
his wish to build a temple, and Gessen wished to
complete this temple for him.

After Gessen had accomplished his three
wishes, he threw away his brushes and artist's
materials and, retiring to the mountains, never
painted again.

48

ACCURATE PROPORTION

Sen-No Rikyu, a tea master, wished to hang
a flower-basket on a column. He asked a carpenter
to help him, directing the man to place it a little
higher, or lower, to the right or left, until he
had found exactly the right spot. "That's the
place," said Sen-No-Rikyu finally.

The carpenter, to test the master, marked the
spot, and then pretended he had forgotten. Was
this the place? "Was this the place, perhaps?"

the carpenter kept asking, pointing to various places on the column.

But os accurate was the tea master's sense of proportion that it was not until the carpenter reached the identical spot again that its location was approved.

49

BLACK-NOSED BUDDHA

A nun who was searching for enlightenment made a statue of Buddha and covered it with gold leaf. Wherever she went she carried this golden Buddha with her.

Years passed and, still carrying her Buddha, the nun came to live in a small temple in a country where there were many Buddhas, each one with its own particular shrine.

The nun wished to burn incense before her golden Buddha. Not liking the idea of the perfume straying to the others, she devised a funnel through which the smoke would ascend only to her statue. This blackened the nose of the golden Buddha, making it especially ugly.

50

RYO-NEN'S CLEAR REALIZATION

The Buddhist nun, known as Ryo-Nen, was
born in 1797. She was a granddaughter of the
famous Japanese warrior, Shingen. Her poetical
genius and alluring beauty were such that at
seventeen she was serving the Empress as one of
the ladies of the Court. Even at such a youthful
age fame awaited her.

The beloved Empress died suddenly and Ryo-Nen's
hopeful dreams vanished. She became acutely aware
of the impermanency of life in this world. It was
then that she desired to study Zen.

Her relatives however, disagreeing, practically
forced her into marriage. With a promise that she
might become a nun after she had borne three children
Ryo-Nen assented. Before she wastwenty-five she had
accomplished this condition. Then her husband and
relatives could no longer dissuade her from her
desire. She shaved her head, took the name of
Ryo-Nen, which means to realize clearly, and started
on her pilgrimage.

She came to the city of Edo, and asked Tetsu-

Gyu to accept her as a disciple. At one glance
the master rejected her because she was too
beautiful.

Ryo-Nen then went to another master, Haku-Wo
Haku-Wo refused her for the same reason, saying
that her beauty would only make trouble.

Ryo-Nen obtained a hot iron and placed it
against her face. In a few moments her beauty
had vanished for ever.

Haku-Wo then accepted her as a disciple.

Commemorating this occasion, Ryo-Nen wrote
a poem on the back of a little mirror.

In the service of my Empress I burned incense
to perfume my exquisite clothes,
Now as a homeless mendicant I burn my face to
enter a Zen temple.

When Ryo-Nen was about to pass from this
world, she wrote another poem.

Sixty-six times have these eyes beheld the
changing scene of Autumn.
I have said enough about moonlight,
Ask no more.
Only listen to the voice of pines and cedars
when on wind stirs.

51

SOUR MISO

The cook monk, Dia-Ryo, at Ban-Kei's monastery
~~decided~~ that he would take good care of his old
teacher's health and give him only fresh miso,
a paste of soy beans mixed with wheat and yeast
that often ferments. Ban-Kei noticing that he was
being served better miso ~~than~~ his pupils asked,
"Who is the cook to-day?"

Dai-Ryo was sent before him. Ban-Kei learned
that according to his age and position he should
eat only fresh miso. So he said to the cook,
"Then you think I shouldn't eat at all."
With this he entered his room and locked the door.

Dai-Ryo, sitting outside the door, asked his
teacher's pardon. Ban-Kei would not answer.
For seven days Dai-Ryo sat outside, and Ban-Kei
within.

Finally in desperation an adherent called
loudly to Ban-Kei, "You may be all right, old
teacher, but this young disciple here has to eat.
He cannot go without food for ever!"

At that Ban-Kei opened the door. He was

smiling. He told Dai-Ryo, "I insist on eating
the same food as the least of my followers. When
you become the teacher, I do not want you to
forget this."

52

YOUR LIGHT MAY GO OUT

A student of Tendai, a philosophical school,
came to the Zen abode of Ga-San as a pupil. When
he was departing a few years later, Ga-San warned
him, "Studying the trut speculatively is useful
as a way of collecting preaching material. But
remember that unless you meditate constantly,
your light of truth may go out."

53

THE GIVER SHOULD BE THANKFUL

While Sei-Setsu was the master of Engaku in
Kamakura, he required larger quarters, since those
in which he was teaching were overcrowded. Umezu
Sei-Bei, a merchant of Edo, decided to donate

five hundred ryo toward the construction of a
more commodious school. This money he brought
to the teacher in gold.

Sei-Setsu said, "All right, I will take it."

Umezu gave Sei-Setsu the sack of gold, but he
was dissatisfied with the attitude of the teacher.
One might live a whole year on three ryo, and
the merchant had not even been thanked for five
hundred.

"In that sack is five hundred ryo," hinted
Umezu.

"You told me that before," replied Sei-Setsu.

"Even if I am a wealthy merchant, five hundred
ryo is a lot of money," said Umezu.

"Do you want me to thank you for it?" asked
Sei-Setsu.

"You ought to," replied Umezu.

"Why should I?" inquired Sei-Setsu. "The giver
should be thankful."

54

THE LAST WILL AND TESTAMENT

Ikkyu, a famous Zen teacher of the Ashikaga
eram was the son of the Emperor. When he was

very young, his mother left the palace and want to
study Zen in a temple. In this way Prince Ikkyu
also became a student. When his mother passed on,
she left with him a letter. It read:

TO IKKYU:

I have finished my work in this life and am
now returning into Eternity. I wish you to
become a good student and to realize your Buddha-
nature. You will know if I am in hell, and whether
I am always with you or not.

If you become a man who realizes that the
Buddha and his follower, Bodhi-dharma, are your
own servants, you may leave off studying and work
for humanity. The Buddha preached for forty-nine
years, and in all that time found it not necessary
to speak one word. You ought to know why. But
if you don't yet wish to, avoid thinking fruitlessly.

> Your Mother,
> Not born, not dead
> September first.

P.S. - The teaching of Buddha was mainly for the
purpose of enlightening others. If you are

dependent on any of its methods, you are naught
but an ignorant insect. There are 80,000 books
on Buddhism and if you should read all of them
and then not see your own nature, you will not
understand even this letter. This is my will
and testament.

55

THE TEA MASTER AND THE ASSASSIN

Taiko, a warrior who lived in Japan before
the Tokugawa era, studied Cha-no-yu, tea
etiquette, with Sen-No-Rikyu, a teacher of that
aesthetical expression of calmness and contentment.

Taiko's attendant warrior, Kato, interpreted
his superior's enthusiasm for tea etiquette as
negligence of the State's affairs, so he decided
to kill Sen-No-Rikyu. He pretended to make a
social call upon the tea master, and was invited
to drink tea.

The master, who was well skilled in his art,
saw at a glance the warrior's intension, so he
invited Kato to leave his sword outside before

entering the room for the ceremony, explaining
that Cha-no-yu represents peacefulness itself.

Kato would not listen to this. "Iaam a
warrior," he said. "I always have my sword
with me. Cha-no-yu or no Cha-no-yu, I have my
sword."

"Very well. Bring your sword in and have
some tea," consented Sen-No Rikyu.

The kettle was boiling on the charcoal fire.
Suddenly Sen-No Rikyu tipped it over. Hissing
steam arose, filling the room with smoke and
ashes. The startled warrior ran outside.

The tea master apologized. "It was my mistake.
Come back in and have some tea. I have your
sword here covered with ashes, and will clean it
and give it to you."

In this predicatment the warrior realized
he could not very well kill the tea master, so he
gave up the idea.

56

THE TRUE PATH

Just before Ninakawa passed away, the Zen
master Ikkyu visited him. "Shall I lead you on?"
Ikkyu asked.

Ninakawa replied, "I came here alone and I
go alone. What help could you be to me?"

Ikkyu answered, "If you think you really
come and go, that is your delusion. Let me show
you the path on which there is no coming and no
going."

With his words, Ikkyu had revealed the path
so clearly that Ninakawa smiled and passed away.

57

THE GATES OF PARADISE

A soldier named Nobu-Shige came to Haku-In
and asked, "Is there really a paradise and a hell?"

"Who are you?" inquired Haku-In.

"I am a Samurai," the warrior replied.

"You, a soldier!" exclaimed Haku-In.

"What kind of ruler would have you as his guard?
Your face looks like that of a beggar."

Nobu-Shige became so angry that he began to
draw his sword when Haku-In continued, "So you have
a sword! Your weapon is probably much too dull
to cut off my head."

As Nobu-Shige drew his sword Haku-In
remarked, "Here open the gates of hell!"

At these words the Samurai perceiving the
master's discipli e sheathed his sword and bowed.

"Here open the gates of paradise," said
Haku-In.

58

ARRESTING THE STONE BUDDHA

A merchant bearing fifty rolls of cotton goods
on his shoulders stopped to rest from the heat
of the day beneath a shelter where a large stone
Buddha was standing. He there fell asleep and
when he awoke his goods had disappeared. He
immediately reported the matter to the police.

A judge named O-Lka opened court oto investi-
gate. "That stone Buddha must have stolen the
goods," concluded the judge. "He is supposed
to care for the welfare of the poeple, but he has
failed to perform his holy duty. Arrest him."

The police arrested the stone Buddha and
carried it into the court. A noisy crowd followed
the statue, curious to learn what kind of a
sentence the judge was about to impose.

When O-Oka appeared on the Bench he rebuked
the bo sterous audience. "What right have you
people to appear before the c ourt laughing and
joking in this manner? You are in contempt of
court and subject to a fine and imprisonment."

The people hastened to apologize. "I shall
have to impose a fine on you," said the judge,
"but I will remit it provided each one of you
brings one roll of cotton goods to the court within
three days. Anyone failing to do this will be
arrested."

Within that time the thief was located easily.
The merchant recovered his goods, and the cotton
rolls were returned to the people.

59

SOLDIERS OF HUMANITY

Once the Osaka Division of the Japanese Army
was engaged in a sham battle. Some of the offibers
found it necessary to make their headquarters in
Ga-San's temple.

All Japanese are patriots, and army men are

usually treated very well. But Ga-San told his
cook, "Let the officers have only the same simple
fare we eat."

This made the army men angry. One came to
Ga-San and said, "Who do you think we are? We
are soldiers, sacrificing our lives for our
country. Why don't you treat us accordingly?"

Ga-San answered sternly, "Who do you think
we are? We are soldiers of humanity, aiming to
save all sentient beings."

60

THE TUNNEL

Zen-Kai, the son of a Samurai, journeyed to
Edo and there became the subject of a high official.
He fell in love with official's wife and was
discovered. In self-defence, he slew the official.
Then he ran away with the wife.

Both of them later became thieves. But the
woman was so greedy that Zen-Kai grew disgusted.
Finally, leaving her, he journeyed far away to the
state of Buzen where he became a wandering mendicant.

To atone for his past, Zen-Kai resolved to
accomplish some good deed in his lifetime.
Knowing of a dangerous road over a cliff, causing
the death and injury of many persons, he resolved
to cut a tunnel through the mountain there.

Begging food in the daytime, Zen-Kai worked
at night, digging his tunnel. When thirty years
had gone by the tunnel was 2280 feet long, 20 feet
high, and 30 feet wide.

Two years before the work was completed, the
son of the official he had slain, who was a
skillful swordsman, found Zen-Kai out and came
to kill him in revenge.

"I will give you my life willingly," said
Zen-Kai. "Only let me finish this work. On the
day it is completed, then you may kill me."

So the son awaited the day. Several months
passed and Zen-Kai kept on digging. The son
grew tired of doing nothing and began to help with
the digging. After he had assisted Zen-Kai for
more than a year, he came to admire his strong wil
and character.

At last the tunnel was completed and the
people could use it and travel in safely.

"Now cut off my head," said Zen-Kai. "My
work is done."

"How can I cut off my own teacher's head?"
asked the younger man with tears in his eyes.

61

GU-DO AND THE EMPEROR

The Emperor Goyosei was studying Zen under
Gu-Do. He inquired, "In Zen this very mind
is Buddha. Is this correct?"

Gu-Do answered, "If I say, Yes, you will think
that you understand without understanding. If
I say, No, I would be contradicting a fact which
many understand quite well."

On another day the Emperor asked Gu-Do,
"Where does the enlightened man go when he dies?"

Gu-Do answered, "Iknow not."

"Why don't you know?" asked the Emperor.

"Because I have not died yet," replied
Gu-Do.

The Emperor hesitated to inquire further about
these things his mind could not grasp. So Gu-Do
beat the floor with his hand as if to awaken him
and the Emperor was enlightened!

The Emperor respected Zen and old Gu-Do
more than ever after his enlightenment, and he
even permitted Gu-Do to wear his hat in the
palace in winter. When Gu-Do was over eighty,
he used to fall asleep in the midst of his lecture,
and the Emperor would quietly retire to another
room so his beloved teacher might enjoy the rest
his aging body required.

62

IN THE HANDS OF DESTINY

A great Japanese warrior named Nobunaga
decided to attack the enemy although hehad
only one-tenth the number of menthe opposition
commanded. He knew that he would win, but his
soldiers were in doubt.

On the way he stopped at a Shinto shrine and
told his men, "After I visit the shrine, I will toss
a coin. If heads comes we will win, if tails we
will lose. Destiny holds us in her hand."

Nobunaga entered the shrine and offered a
silent prayer. He came forth and tossed a coin.

Heads appeared. His soldiers were so eager to
fight that they won their battle easily.

"no one can change the hand of destiny," his
attendant told him after the battle.

"Indeed not," said Nobunaga, showing a coin
which had been doubled, with the two heads facing
the outside.

63

KILLING

Ga-San instructed his adherents one day:
"Those who speak against killing and who desire
to spare the lives of all conscious beings are
right. It is good to protect even animals and
insects. But what about those persons who kill
time, what aboutthose who are destroying wealth,
and those who destroy political economy? We should
not overlook them. Furthermore, what of the one wh
who
who preaches without enlightenment? He is killing
Buddhism."

64

KA-SAN SWEAT

Ka-San was asked to officiate at the funeral
of a provincial lord.

He had never met lords and nobles before, so
was nervous. When the ceremony started Ka-Sam
sweat.

Afterwards when he had returned he gathered
his pupils together. Ka-San confessed that he
was not yet qualified to be a teacher, for he
lacked the sameness of bearing in the world of
fame that he possessed in the secluded temple.
Then Ka-San resigned and became the pupil of
another master. Eight years later he returned to
his former pupils, enlightened.

65

THE SUBJUGATION OF A GHOST

A young wife fell sick and was about to die.
"I love you so much, " she told her husband,

"I do not want to leave you. Do not go from
me to any other woman. If you do, I will return
as a ghost and cause you endless trouble."

Soon the wife passed away. The husband respected
her last wish for the first three months, but
then he met another woman and fell in love with her.
They became engaged to be married.

Immediately after the engagement, a ghost
appeared every night to the man, blaming his for
not keeping his promise. The ghost was clever too
She told him exactly what had transpired between
himself and his new sweetheart. Whenever he gave
his fiancee a present, the ghost would describe
it in detail. She would even repeat conversations
and it so annoyed the man that he could not sleep.
Someone advised him to take his problem to a Zen
master who lived close to the village. At length,
in despair, the poor man want to him for help.

"Your former wife became a ghost and knows
everything you do," commented the master.
"Whatever you do or say, whatever you give your
beloved, she knows. She must be a very wise ghost.
Really you should admire such a ghost. The next
time she appears, bargain with her. Tell her that
she knows so much you can hide nothing from her,
and that if she will answer you one question,

you promise to break your engagement and remain single."

"What is the question I must ask her?" inquired the man.

The master replied, "Take a large handful of soy beans, and ask her exactly how many beans you hold in your hand. If she cannot tell you, you will know she is only a figment of your imagination and will trouble you no longer."

The next night when the ghost appeared, the man flattered her and told her that she knew everything.

"Indeed," replied the ghost," and I know you went to see that Zen master to-day."

"And since you know so much," demanded the man, "tell me how many beans I hold in this hand!"

There was no longer any ghost to answer the question.

66

CHILDREN OF HIS MAJESTY

Yamaoka Tesshu was a tutor of the Emperor. He was also a master of fencing, and a profound student of Zen.

His home was the abode of vagabonds. He
had but one suit of clothes, for they kept him
poor.

The Emperor, observing how worn his garments
were, gave Yamaoka some money to buy new ones.
The next time Yamaoka appeared he wore the same
old outfit.

"What became of the new clothes, Tamaoka?"
asked the Emperor.

"I provided clothes for the children of
Your Majesty," explained Yamaoka.

67

WWHAT ARE YOU DOING!   WHAT
ARE YOU SAYING !

In modern times a great deal of nonsense is
talked about maste s and disciples, and the
inheritance of a master's teaching by favorite
pupils, entitling them to apss the truth on the
their adherents. Of course Zen should be imparted
in this way, from heart ot heart, and in the past
it was really accomplished. Silence and humility
reigned rather that profession and assertion.

The one who received such a teaching kept the matter
hidden even after twenty years. Not until another
discovered through his own need that a real master
was at hand, was it learned that the teaching had
been imparted, and even then the occasion arose
quite naturally and the teaching made its way in
its own right. Under no circumstance did the
teacher ever claim, "I am the successor of So-and
So." Such a claim would prove quite the contrary.

The Zen master, Mu-Nan, had only one successor.
His name was Sho-Ju. After Sho-Ju had completedd
his study of Zen, Mu-Nan called him into his room.
"I am getting old," he said, "and as far as I know
Sho-Ju, you are the only one who will cary on this
teaching. Here is a book. It has been passed down
from master to master for seven generations. I also
have added many points according to my understanding.
The book is very valuable, and I am giving it to
you to represent your successorship."

"If the book is such an important thing, you
had better keep it," Sho-Mu replied. "I received
your Zen without writing and am satisfied with it
as it is."

"I know that," said Mu-Nan. "Even so, this work
was carried from master to master, for seven

generations, so you may keep it as a symbol
of having received the teaching. Here."

The two happened to be talking befor a stove.
The instant Sho-Ju felt the book in his hands,
he thrust it inot the flames. He had nolust
for poss█████ions.

Mu-Nan, who never had been angry before,
yelled, "What are you doing!"

Sho-Ju shouted back, "What are you saying!"

68

ONE NOTE OF ZEN

After Kaku-A visited the Emperor he disappeared and no one knew what became of him.
He was the first ʋapanese to study Zen in China,
but since he showed nothing of it, save one note,
he is not remembered for having brought Zen into
his country.

Kaku-A visited China and accepted the true
teaching. He did not travel while he was there
Meditating constantly, he lived in a remote part

of a mountain. Whenever people found him and asked him to preach, he would say a few words and then move to another part of the mountain where he could be found less easily.

The Emperor heard about Kaku-A when he returned to Japan, and asked him to preach Zen for his edification and that of his subjects.

Kaku-A stood before the Emperor in silence. He then produced a flute from the folds of his robe, and blew one short note. Bowing politely, he disappeared.

69

EATING THE BLAME

Circumstances arose one day which delayed preparation of the dinner of a Soto Zen master, Fu-Gwai, and his followers. In haste the cook went to the garden with his curved knife and cut off the tops of green vegetables, chopped them together, and made soup, unaware that in his haste he had included a part of a snake in the vegetables.

The followers of Fu-Gwai tho ght they never had tasted such good soup. But when the master himself found the snake's head in his bowl, he summoned the cook. "What is this?" he demanded holding up the head of the snake.

"Oh, thank you, master, replied the cook, taking the morsel and eating it quickly.

70

THE MOST VALUABLE THING IN THE WORLD

So-Zan, a Chinese Zen master, was asked by a student, "What is the most valuable thing in the world?"

The master replied, "The head of a dead cat"

"Why is the head of a dead cat the most val able thing in the world?" inquired the student.

So-Zan replied, "Because no one can name its price."

71

LEARNING TO BE SILENT

The pupils of the Tendai school used to sutdy meditation before Zen entered Japan. Four of them, who were intimate friends, promised one another to observe seven days of silence.

On the first day all were silent. Their meditation had begun auspiciously, but when night came and the oil lamps were growing dim one of the pupils could not help exclaiming to a servant, "Fix those lamps."

The second pupil was surprised to hear the first one talk. "We are not supposed to say a word," he remarked.

"You two are stupid. Why did you talk?" asked the third.

"I am the only one who has not talked," concluded the fourth pupil.

72

the BLOCKHEAD LORD

Two Zen teachers, Dai-Gu and Gu-Do, were invited to visit a lord. Upon arriving Gu-Do said to the lord, "You are wise by nature, and have an inborn ability to learn Zen."

"Nonsense," said Dai-Gu. "Why do you flatter this blockhead? He may be a lord, but he doesn't know anyting of Zen."

So instead of building a temple ofor Gu-Do, the lord built it for Dai-Gu andstudied Zen with him.

73

TEN SUCCESSORS

Zen pupils take a vow that even if they are killed by their teacher, they intend to learn Zen. Usually they cut a finger and seal their resolution with blood. In time the vow has become a mere formality, and for this reason the pupil who died by the hand of Eki-Do was made to appear a martyr.

Eki-Do had become a severe teacher. His pupils feared him. One of them on duty, striking the gong to tell the time of day, missed his beats when his eye was attracted by a beautiful girl passing the temple gate.

At that moment, Eki-Do, who was directly behind him, hit him with a stick, and the shock happened to kill him.

The pupil's guardian, hearing of the accident went directly to Eki-Do. Knowing that he was not to blame, he praised the master for his severe teaching. Eki-Do's attitude was just the same as if the pupil were still alive.

After this took place, he was able to produce under his guidance more that ten enlightened successors, a very unusual number.

74

TRUE REFORMATION

Ryo-Kwan devoted his life to the study of Zen. One day he heard that his nephew, despite,

the admonitions of relatives, was spending his
money on a courtesan. Inasmuch as the nephew
had taken Ryo-Kwan's place in managing the family
estate, and the property was in danger of being
dissipated, the relatives asked Ryo-Kwan to do
something about it.

Ryo-Kwan had to travel a long way to visit
his nephew whom he had not seen for many years.
The nephew seemed pleased to meet his uncle again,
and invited him to remain overnight.

All night Ryo-Kwan sat in meditation. As he
was departing in themorning he said to the young
man, "I must be getting old, my hand shakes so.
Will you help me tie the string of my straw
sandal?"

The nephew helped him willingly. "Thank
you, finished Ryo-Kwan, "you see, a man becomes
older and feeble day by day. Take good care of
yourself." Then Ryo-Kwan left, never mentioning a
word about the courtesan or the complaints of the
relatives. But from that morning on the dissipations
of the nephew ended.

75

TEMPER

A Zen student came to Ban-Kei and complained "Master, I have an ungovernable temper. How can I cure it?"

"You have something very strange," replied Ban-Kei. "Let me see what you have."

"Just now I cannot show it to you," replied the other.

"When can you show it to me?" asked Ban-Kei.

"It arises unexpectedly," replied the student.

"Then," concluded Ban-Kei, "it must not be your own true nature. If it were, you could show it to me at any time. When you were born you did not have it, and your parents did not give it otto you. Think that over."

76

the STONE MIND

Ho-Gen, a Chinese Zen teacher, lived alone in a samll temple in the country. One day four travellingmonks appeared and asked if they might make a fire in his yard to warm themselves.

While they were building the fire, Ho-Gen heard them arguing about subjectivity and objectivity. He joined them and said, "There is a big stone. Do you consider it to inside or outside your mind?"

One of the monks replied, "From the Buddhist viewpoint everytins is an objectification of mind, so I would say that the stone is inside my mind."

"Your head must feel very heavy," observed Ho-Gen, "if you are carrying around a stone like that in your mind."

77

NO ATTACHMENT FOR DUST

Zen-Getsu, a Chinese master of the Tang dynasty, wrote the following advice for his pupils:

Living in the world yet not forming attachments for the dust tof the world, is the way of a true Zen student.

When witnessing the good action of another, encourage yourself to follow his example. Hearing of the mistaken action of another, advise yourself not to emulate it.

Even though alone in a dark room, be as if you were facing a noble guest. Express your feelings, but become no more expressive than your tru nature.

Poverty is your treasure. Never exchange it for an easy life.

A person may appear like a fool and yet be not one. He may only be quarding his wisdom carefully.

Virtues are the fruit of self-discipline and do not drop from heaven of themselves like rain or snow.

Modesty is the foundation of all virtues. Let your neighbours discover you before you make yo rself known to them.

A noble heart never forces itself forward. Its words are as rare g ms, seldom displayed and of great value.

To a sincere sutdent, every day is a fortunate day. Time passes but he never lags behind. Neither glory nor shame can move him.

Censur yourself, never another. Do not discuss right and wrong.

Some things, though right, were considered
wrong for generations. Since the value of right-
eousness may be recognized after centuries, there
is no need to crave an immediate appreciation.

Live with cause and leave results to the
great law of the universe. Pass each day in
peaceful comtemplation.

78
REAL PROSPERITY

A rich man asked Sen-Gai to write something
for the continued prosperity of his family so
that it might be treasured from generation to
generation.

Sen-Gai obtained a large sheet of paper
and wrote: "Father dies, son dies, grandson dies."

The rich man became angry. "I asked you
to write something for the happiness of my
family! Why do you make such a joke as this?"

No joke is intended," explained Sen-Gai.
"If before you die your son should die, this
would grieve you greatly. If your grandson
should pass away before your son, both of you

would be broken-hearted. If your family, generation after gene ation, passes away in the order I have named, it will be the natural course of life. I call this real prosperity."

79

INCENSE BURNER

A woman of Nagasaki, named Kame, was one of the few makers of incense burners in Japan. Such a burner is a work of art to be used only in a tea room or before a family shrine.

Kame, whose father before her had been such an artist, was fond of drinking. She also smoked and associated with men most of the time. Whenever she made a little money she gave a feast inviting artists, poets, carpenters, workers, all men of many vocations and avocations. In their association she evolved her designs.

Kame was exceedingly slow in creating, but when her work was finished it was always a masterpiece. Her burners were treasured in homes whose womenfolk never drank, smoked or associated freely with men.

The mayor of Nagasaki once requested Kame to design an incense burner for him. She delayed to do so until almost half a year had passed. At that time the mayor, who had been promoted to office in a distant city, visited her. He urged Kame to begin work on his burner.

At last receiving the inspiration, Kame made the incense burner. After it was completed, she placed it upon a table. She looked at it long and carefully. She smoked and drank before it as if it were her own company. All day she observed it.

At last, picking up a hammer, Kame smashed it to bits. She saw it was not the perfect creation her mind demanded.

80

THE REAL MIRACLE

When Ban-Kei was preaching at Ryu-Mon temple, a Shin-Shu priest, who believed in salvation through the repetition fo the name of the Buddha of Love, was jealous of his large audience and wanted to debate with him.

Ban-Kei was in the midst of a talk when the priest appeared, but the fellow made such a disturbance that he stopped his discourse and asked about the noise.

"The founder of our sect," boasted the priest, "had such miraculous powers that he held a brush in his hand on one bank of the river, and his attendant held up a paper on the other bank, while the teacher wrote the holy name of Amida throught the air. Can you do such a wonderful thing?"

Ban-Kei replied lightly, "Perhaps your fox can perform that trick, but that is not the manner of Zen. My miracle is that when I feel hungry I eat, and when I feel thirsty I drink."

81

JUST GO TO SLEEP

Ga-San was sitting at the bedside of Teki-Sui three days before his teacher's passing. Teki-Sui had already chosen him as his successor.

A temple recently had burned, and Ga-San was busy rebuilding the structure. Teki-Sui asked him,

"What are you going to do when you get the temple rebuilt?"

"When your sickness is over, we want you to speak there," siad Ga-San.

"Suppose I do not live until then?" aksed the teacher.

"Then we will get someone elso," replied Ga-San.

"Suppose you cannot find anyone?" continued Teki-Sui.

Ga-San answered loudly, "Don't ask such foolish questions. Just go to sleep.

82

NOTHING EXISTS

Yamaoka Tesshu as a young student of Zen visited one master after another. He called upon Doku-On of Shokoku.

Desiring to show his attainment, he said, "The mind, Buddha, and sentient beings, after all, do not exist. The true nature of phenomena is emptiness. There is no realization, no delusion,

no sage, no mediocrity. There is no giving and
nothing to be received."

Doku-On, who was smoking quietly, said
nothing. Suddenly he whacked Yamaoka with his
bamboo pipe. This made the youth quite angry.

"If nothing exists," inquired Doku-On,
"where did this anger come from?"

83

NO WORK, NO FOOD

Hyaku-Jo, the Chinese Zen master, used to
labour with his pupils even at the age of eightly
trimming the gardens, cleaning the grounds and prun-
ing the trees.

The pupils felt sorry to see the old teacher
working so hard, but they knew he would not
listen to their advice to stop, so they hid away
his tools.

That day the master did not eat. The next
day he did not eat, nor the next. "He may be
angry because we have hidden his tools," the

pupils surmised.   "We had better put them back."

The day they did, the teach worked and ate the same as before. In the evening he instructed them, "No work, no food."

84

TRUE FRIENDS

A long time ago in China there were two friends, one who played the harp skillfully and one who listened skilfully.

When the one played or sang about a mountain, the other would say, "I can see the mountain before us."

When the one played about water, the listener would exclaim, "Here is the running stream!"

But the listener fell sick and died. The first friend cut the strings of his harp and never played again. Since that time the cutting of harp strings has always been a sign of intimate friendship.

85

TIME TO DIE

Ikkyu, the Zen master, was very clever even
as a boy. His teacher had a precious tea cup, a
rare antigue. Ikkyu happened to break this cup
and wasgreatly perplexed. Hearing the footsteps
of his teacher, he held the peices of the cup
behind him. When the master appeared, Ikkyu
asked, "Why do people have to die?"

"This is natural," explained the older man.
"Eve y thing has to die, and has just so long to
live."

Ikkyu, producing the shattered cup, added,
"It was time for your cup to die."

86

THE LIVING BUDDHA AND THE TUBMAKER

Zen masters give personal guidance in a
secluded room. No one enters while the teacher
and pupil are together.

Moku-Rai, the Zen master of Ken-Nin temple in Kyoto, used to enjoy talking with merchants and newspaper men as well as his pupils. A certain tubmaker also came to see him. The tubmaker was almost illiterate. He would ask foolish questions of Moku-Rai, have tea, and then go away.

One day while the tubmaker was there Moku-Rai wished to give personal guidance to a disciple so he asked the tubmaker to wait in another room.

"I understand you are a living Buddha," the man protested. "Even the stone Buddhas in the temple never refuse the numerous persons who come together before them. Why then should I be excluded?"

Moku-Rai had to go outside to see his disciple.

87

THREE KINDS OF DISCIPLES

A Zen master named Gettan lived in the latter part of the Tolugawa era. He used to say,

"There are three kinds od disciples, those who
impart Zen to others, those who maihtain the
temples and shrines, and them there are the rice-
bags and the clothes hangers."

Ga-San expressed the same idea. When he
wasstudying under Teki-Sui, his teacher was very
sever. Sometimes he even beat him. Other pupils
would not stand this kind of teaching, and quit.
Ga-San remained, saying, "A poor disciple
utilizes a teacher's influence. A fair disciple
admires a teacher's kindness. A goo disciple
grows strong under a teacher's discipline."

88

HOW TO WRITE A CHINESE POEM

A well-known Japanese poet was asked hot
to compose a Chinese poem.

"The usual Chinese poem is four lines," he
explained. "The first line contains the initial
phase, the second line, the continuation of that
phase. The thrid line turns from this subject and
begins a new one, and the fourth line brings

the first three lines together, A popular Japanese
song illustrates this,"

Two daughters of a silk merchant live in Kyoto.
The elder is twenty, the younger, eighteen.
A soldier may kill with his sword,
But these girls slay men with their eyes,

89.

ZEN DIALOGUE

Zen teachers train their young pupils to
express themselves, Two Zen temples each had
a child protege, One child, going to obtain
vegetables each morning, would meet the other on
the way,

"Wh ere are you going?" asked the one,

"I am going wherever my feet go," the other
responded,

This reply puzzled the first child who went
to his teacher for help, "to-morrow morning," the
teacher told him, "when you meet that little fellow
ask him the same question, He will give you the
same answer, and you ask him,

'Suppose you have no feet, then where are you going?' That will fix him."

The children met again the following morning.

"Where are you going?" asked the first child.

"Iam going wherever the wind blows," answered the other.

This again nonplussed the youngster who took his defeat to his teacher.

"Ask him where he is going if there is no wind," suggested the teacher.

The next day the children met a third time.

"Where are you going?" asked the first child.

"I am going to market to buy vegetables," the other replied.

90

THE IA ST RAP

Tan-Gen had studied with Sen-Gai since childhood. When he was twenty he wanted to leave his teacher and visit others for comparptive study, but Sen-Gai would not permit this. Every time Tan-Gen suggested it, Sen-Gai would give him a rap on the head.

Finally Tan-Gen asked an elder brother to coax permission from Sen-Gai, which the brother did and then reported to Tan-Gen, "It is arranged. I have fixed it for you to start on your pilgrimage at once."

Tan-Gen went to Sen-Gai to thank him for his permissi n. The master answered by giving him another rap.

When Tan-Gen related this to his elder brother the other said, "What is the matter? Sen-Gai has no business giving permission and then changing his mind. I will tell him so." And off he went to see the teacher.

"I did not cancel my permission," said Sen-Gai. "I just wished to give him one last smack over the head, for when he returns he will be enlightened and I will not be able to reprimand him again."

91

THE TASTE OF BAN-ZO'S SWORD

Matajuro Yagyu was the son of a famous
swordsman. His father, believing that his so n's
work was too mediocre to anticipate mastership,
disowned him.

So Matajuro went to Mount Futara and there
fo nd the famo s swordsman, Ban-Zo. But
Ban-Zo confirmed the father's judgment. "You
wish to learn swordsmanship under my guidance?"
asked Ban-Zo. "You cannot fulfil the requirements."

"But if I work hard, how many years will it
take me to become a master?" persisted the youth.

"The rest of your life," replied Ban-Zo.

"I cannot wait that long," explained Matajuro

"I am willing to pass through any hardship if
only you will teach me. If I become your devoted
servant, how long might it be?"

"Oh, maybe ten years," Ban-Zo relented.

"My father is getting old, and soon I must
take care of him," continued Matajuro. "If 1

work far more intesively, how long would it take
me?"

"Oh, maybe thirty years," said Ban-Zo.

"Why is that?" asked Matajuro. "First
you say ten and now thirty years. I will undergo
any hardship to master this art in the shortest
time!"

"Well," said Ban-Zo, "in that case youwill
have to remain with me for seventy years. A
man in such a hurry as you ar to get results
seldom learns quickly."

"Very well, " declared the youth, understanding at last he was being rebuked for
impatience, "I agree."

Matajuro was told never to speak of fencing
and never to touch a sword. He cooked for his
master, washed the dishes, made his bed, cleaned
the yard, cared for the garden, without a word
of swordsmanship.

Three years passed. Still Matajuro laboured
on. Thinking of his future, he was sad. He had
not even begun to learn the art to which he had
devoted his life.

But one day Ban-Zo crept up behind him and
gave him a terrific blow with a wooden sword.

The following day when Matajuro was cooking
rice, Ban-Zo again sprang upon him one expectedly.

After that, day and night, Matajuro had to

defend himself from unexpectedthrusts. Not a
moment passed in any day that he did not have
to think of the taste of Ban-Zo's sword.

He learned so rapidly he brought smiles to
the face of his master. Matajuro became the
greatest swordsman in the land.

92

FIRE-POKER ZEN

Haku-In used to tell his pupils about an old
woman who had a tea ship, praising her under-
standi g of Zen. The pupils refused to believe
wh-t he told them, and would go to the tea shop
to find out for themselves.

Whenever the woman saw them coming, she
could tell at once whether they had come for tea
or to look into her grasp of Zen. In the former
case, she would serve them graciously. In th e
latter, she would beckon the pupils to come
behind her screen. The instant they obeyed, she
would strike them with a fire-poker.

Nine out of ten of them could not escape her
beating.

93

STORY-TELLER'S ZEN

Encho was a famous story-teller. His
tales of love stirred the hearts of his listeners.
When he narrated a story of war, it was as if the
listeners themselves were on the field of battle.

One day Encho met Yamaoka Tesshu, a layman
who had almost embraced masterhood in Zen. "I
understand," said Yamaoka, "you are the best
story-teller in our land, and that you make people
cry or laugh at will. Tell me my favourite
story of the Peach Boy. When I was a little
tot I used to sleep beside my mother, and she often
related this legend. In the middle of the story I
would fall asleep. Tell it to me just as my
mother did."

Encho dared not attempt to do this. He
requested time to study. Several months later
he went to Yamaoka and said, "Please give me the
opportunity to tell you the story."

"Some other day," answered Yamaoka.

Encho was keenly disappointed. He studied
further and tried again. Yamaoka rejected him
many times. When Encho would start to talk,

Yamaoka would stop him, saying, "You, are not yet like my mother."

It took Encho five years to be able to tell Yamaoka the legend as his mother had told it to him.

In this way, Yamaoka imparted Zen to Encho.

94

MIDNIGHT EXCURSION

Many pupils were studying meditation under the Zen master, Sen-Gai. One of them used to arise at night, climb over the temple wall, and go to town on a pleasure jaunt.

Sen-Gai, inspecting the dormitory quarters, found this pupil missing one night, and also discovered the high stool he had used to scale the wall. Sen-Gai removed the stool and stood there in its place.

When the wanderer returned, not knowing that Sen-Gai was the stool, he put his feet on the master's head and jumped down into the grounds. Discovering what he had done, he was aghast.

Sen-Gai said, "It is very chilly in the early

morning. Do be careful not to catch cold
yourself."

The pupil never went out at night again.

95

A LETTER TO A DYING MAN

Bassui wrote the following letter to one of his
disciples who was about to die:

"The essence of your mind is not born, so
it will never die. It is not an existence which is
perishable. It is not an emptiness which is
a mere void. It has neither colour nor form.
It enjoys no pleasures and suffers no pains.

"Iknow you are very ill. Like a good Zen
student, you are facing that sickness squarely
You may not know exactly who is suffering, but
question yourself: What is the essence of this
mind? Think only of this. You will need no more.
Covet nothing. Your end which is endless is as
a smowflake dissovling in the pure
air."

96

A DROP OF WATER

A Zen master named Gi-San asked a young
student to bring him a pail of water to cool
his bath.

The student brought the water, and after
cooling the bath, threw on to the ground the little
that was left over.

"You dunce!" the master scolded him.

"Why didn't you give the rest of the water to
the plants? What right have you to waste even a
drop of water in this temple?"

The young student attained Zen in that
instant. He changed his name to Teki-Sui, which
means a drop of water.

97

TEACHING THE ULTIMATE

In early times in Japan, bamboo and paper
lanterns were used with candles inside. A blind

man, visiting a friend one night, was offered a lantern to carry home with him.

"Ido not need a lantern," he said. "Darkness or light is all the same to me."

"I know you do not need a lantern to find your way," his friend replied, "but if you don't have one, someone else may run tinto you. So you must take it."

The blind man started off with the lantern and before he had walked ve·y far someone ran squarely into him. "Look out where you are gling!" heexclaimed to the stranger. "Can't you see this lantern?"

"Your candle has burned out, brother," replied the stranger.

98

NON-ATTACHMENT

Kitano Genpo, abbot of Ei-Hei-Ji, was ninety two years old when he passed away in the year 1933 He endeavoured his whole life not to be attached to anything. As a wandering mendicant when he was twenty, he happened to meet a traveller who

smoked tobacco. As they walked together down
a mountain road, they stopped under a tree to rest.
The traveller offered Kitano a smoke which he
accepted, as he was very hungry at the time.

"How pleasant this smoking is," he commented.
The other gave him an extra pipe and tobacco
and they parted.

Kitano felt, "Such pelasant things may
disturb my meditation. Before this goes too far,
I will stop now." So he threw the smoking outfit
away.

When he was twenty-three years old he
studied I-King, the profoundest doctrine of the
universe. It was winter at the time, and he needed
some heavy clothes. He wrote his teacher who
lived a hundred miles away, telling him of his
need and gave the letter to a traveller to deliver.
Almost the whole winter passed and neither answer
nor clothes arrived. So Kitano resorted to the
prescience of I-King, which also teaches the art of
divination, to determine whether or not his letter
had been miscarried. He found that this had been
the case. A letter afterwards from his teacher
made no mention of clothes.

"If I perform such accurate determinative

work with I-Ki g, I may neglect my meditation,"
felt Kitano. So he gave up this marvellous
teaching and never resorted to its powers again.

When he was twenty-eight, he studied Chinese
calligraphy and poetry. He grew so skilful in
these art that his teacher praised him. Kitano
mused, "If I don't stop now, I'll be a poet,
not a Zen teacher." So he never wrote another
poem.

99
TO-SUI'S VINEGAR

To-Sui was the Zen master who left the
formalism of temples to live under a bridge
with beggars. When he was getting very old,
a friend helped him to earn his living without
begging. He showed To-Sui how to collect rice
and manufacture vinegar from it, and To-Sui did
this until he passed away.

While To-Sui was making vinegar, one of
the beggars gave him a picture of the Buddha.
To-Sui hung it on the wall of his hut and put a
sign beside it.

It read: Mr. Amida Buddha - This little room
is quite narrow. I can bet you remain as a
transient. But don't think I am asking you
to help me to be reborn in your paradise.

100

THE SILENT TEMPLE

Shoichi was a one-eyed teacher of Zen, spark-
ling with enlightment. He taught his disciples
in To-Fuku temple.

Day and night the whole temple stood in
silence. There was no sound at all.

Even the reciting of Sutras was abolished
by the teacher. His pupils had nothing to do but
meditate.

When the master passed away, an old neighbor
heard the ringing of bells and the recitation of
Sutras. Then she knew Shoichi had gone.

101

101

BUDDHA'S ZEN

Buddha said, "I consider the positions of
kings and rulers as that of dust motes. I observe
threasures of gold and gems as so many bricks and
pebbles. I look upon the finest silken robes as
tattered rages. I see myraid worlds of the
universe as small seeds of fruit, and the greatest
lake in India as a drop of ioil on my foot. I
perceive the teachings of the world to be the illusion
of magicians. I discern the highest conseption of
emancipation as a golden brocade in a dream, and
view the holy path of illuminated ones as flowers
appearing in one's eyes. I see meditation as a
pillar of a mountain, Nirvana, as a nightmare
of daytime. I look upon the judgment of right
and wrong as the serpentine dance of a dragon,
and the rise and fall of beliefs as but traces
left by the four seasons."

E N D

CPSIA information can be obtained at www.ICGtesting.com
Printed in the USA
BVOW011114150113

310675BV00019B/899/P